The Celtic Alpahabet Coloring Book for Children: Volume 1

J. K. Kaguri

Hey, welcome to my book.

Here is a page to try out your materials and coloring techniques!

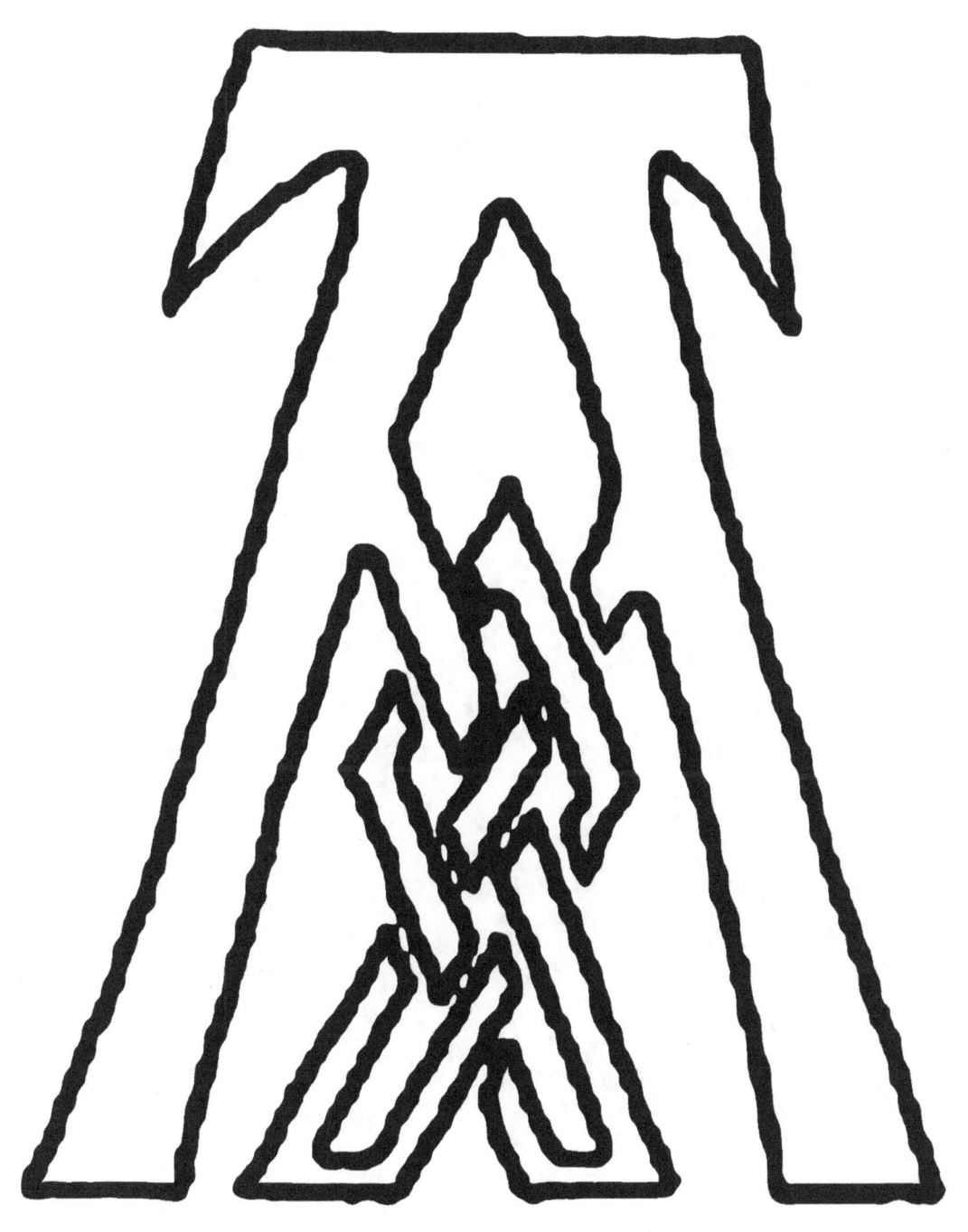

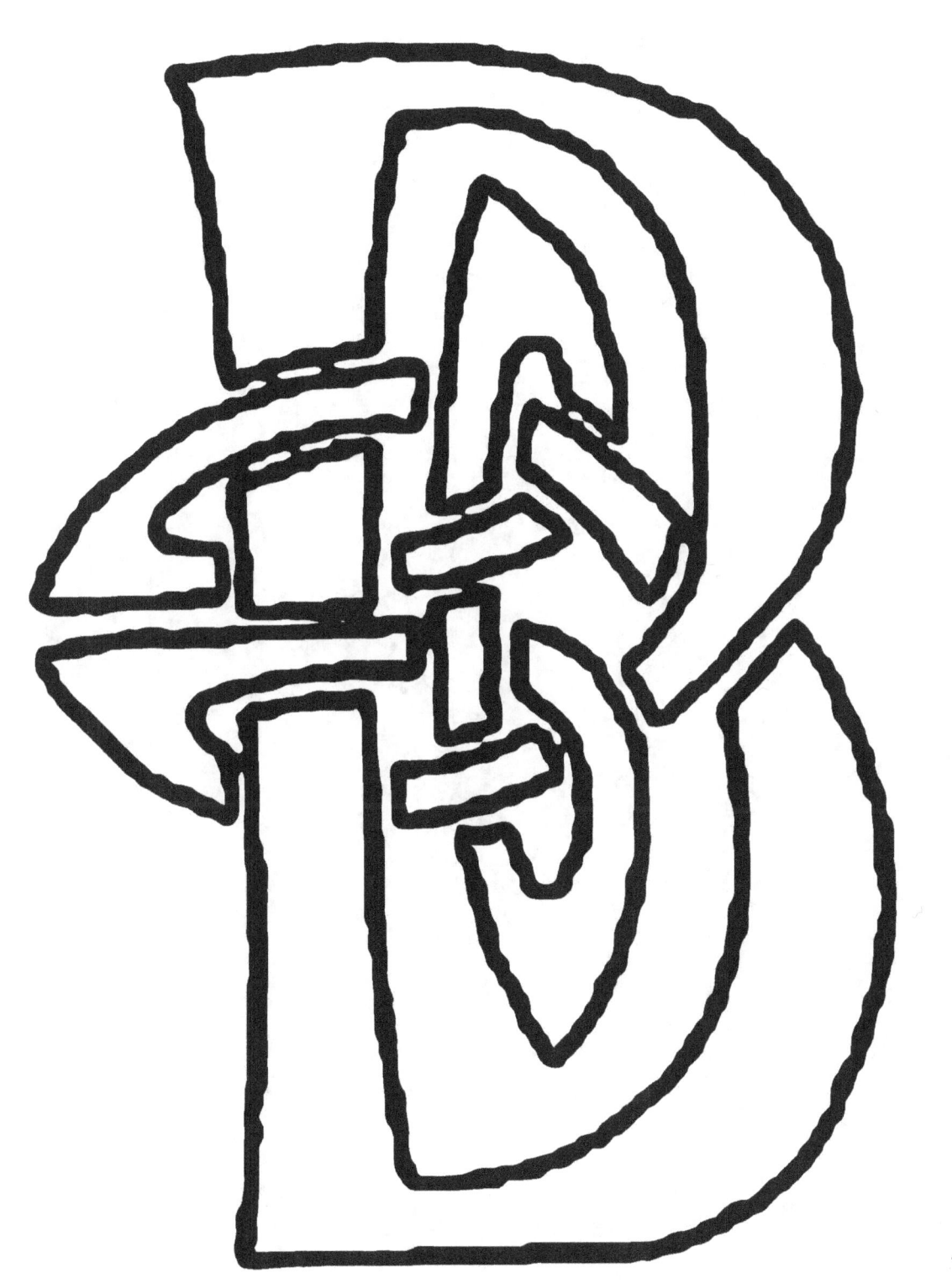

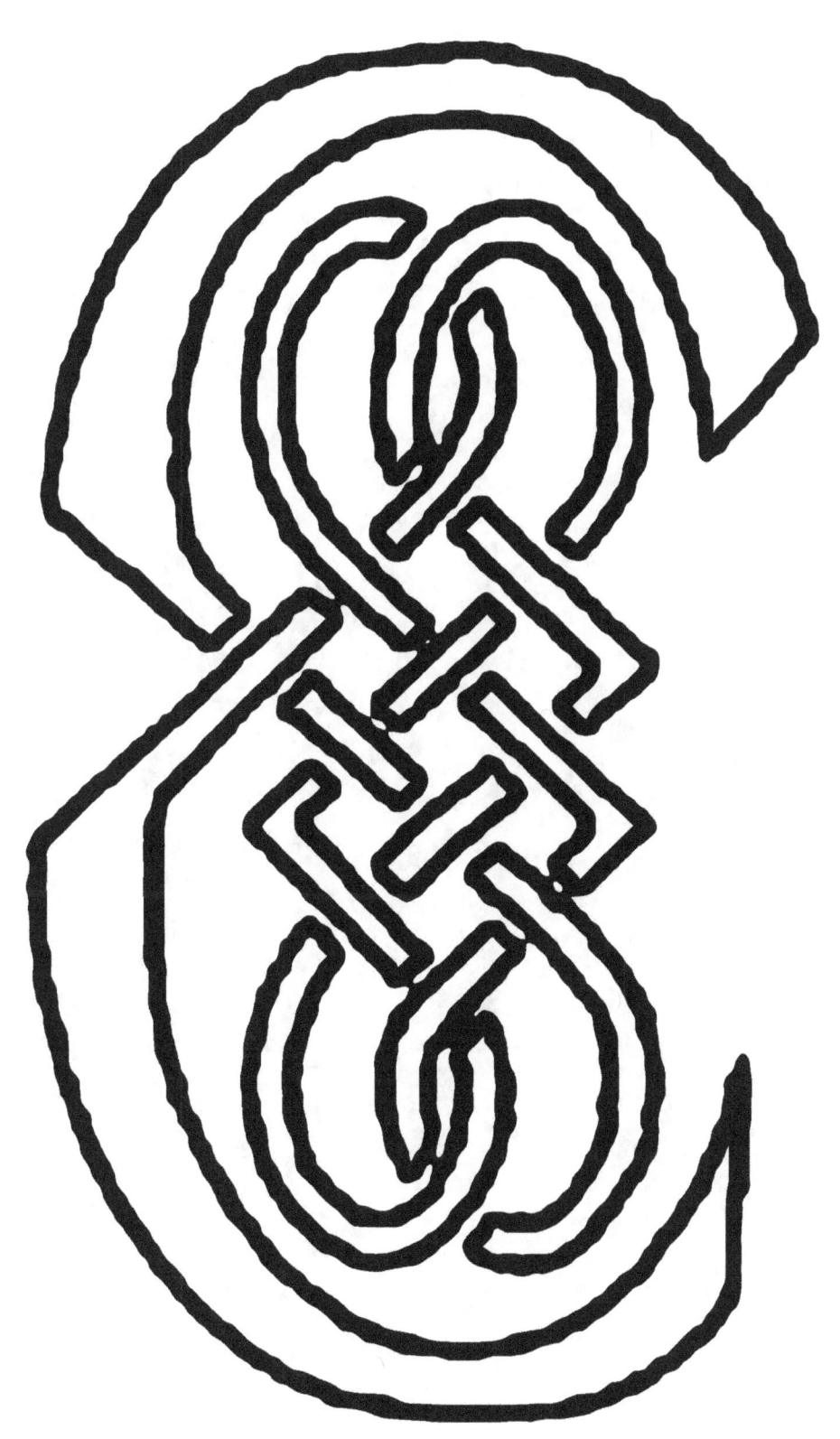

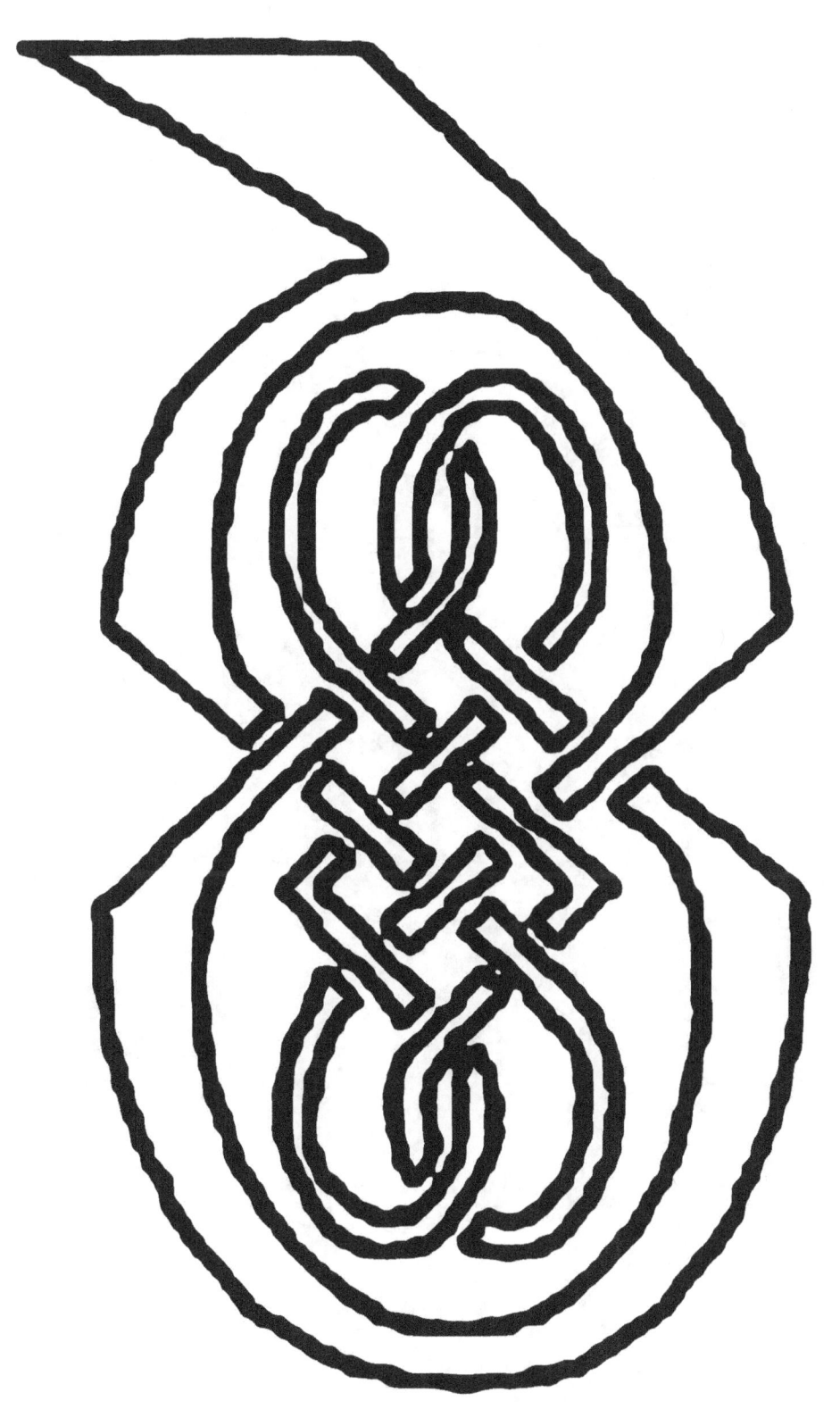

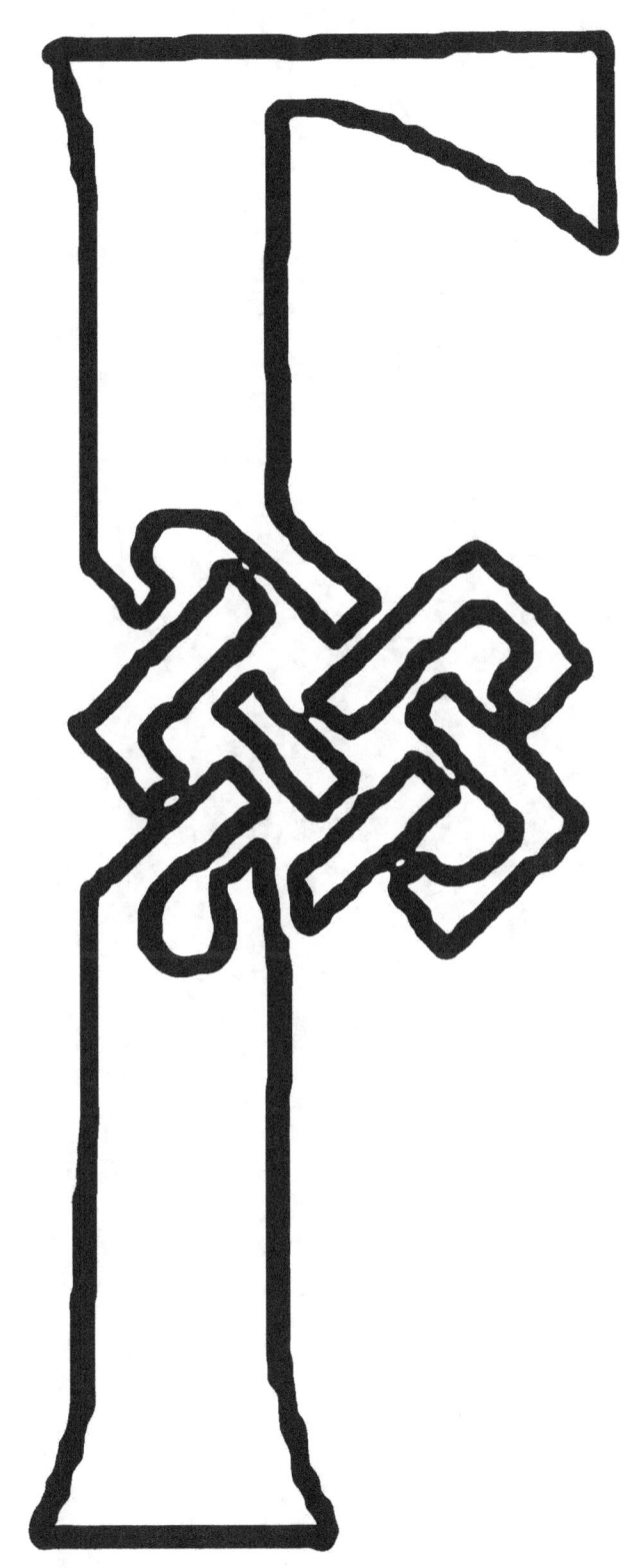

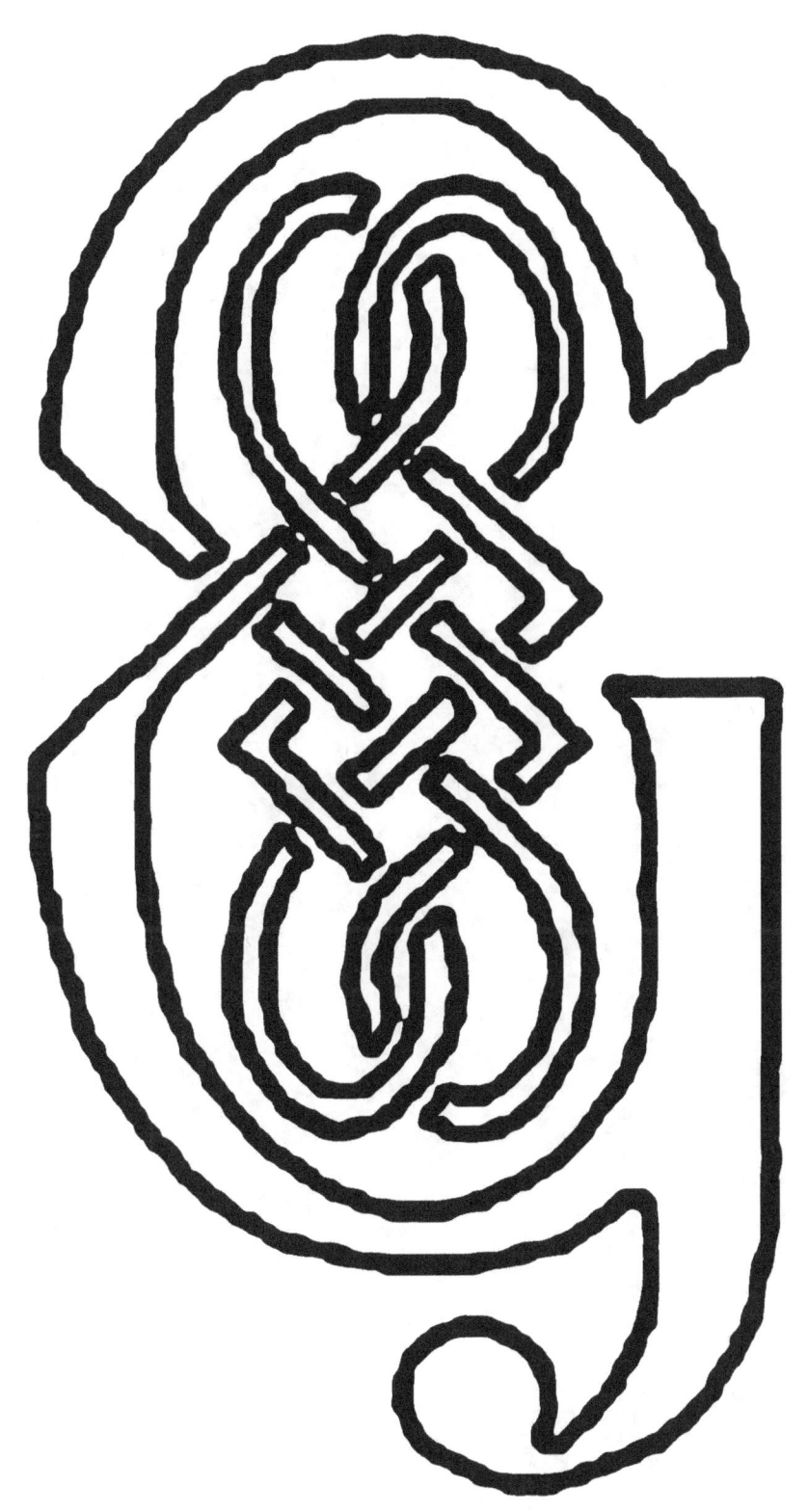

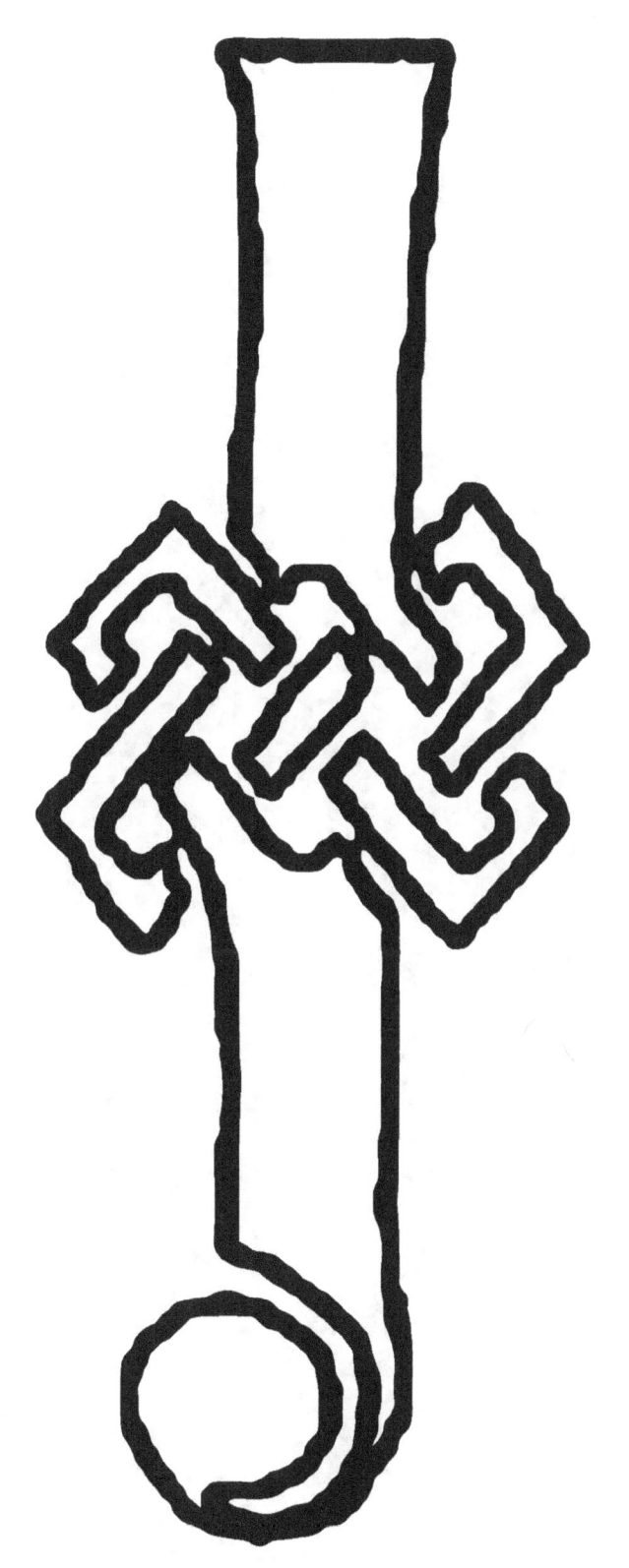

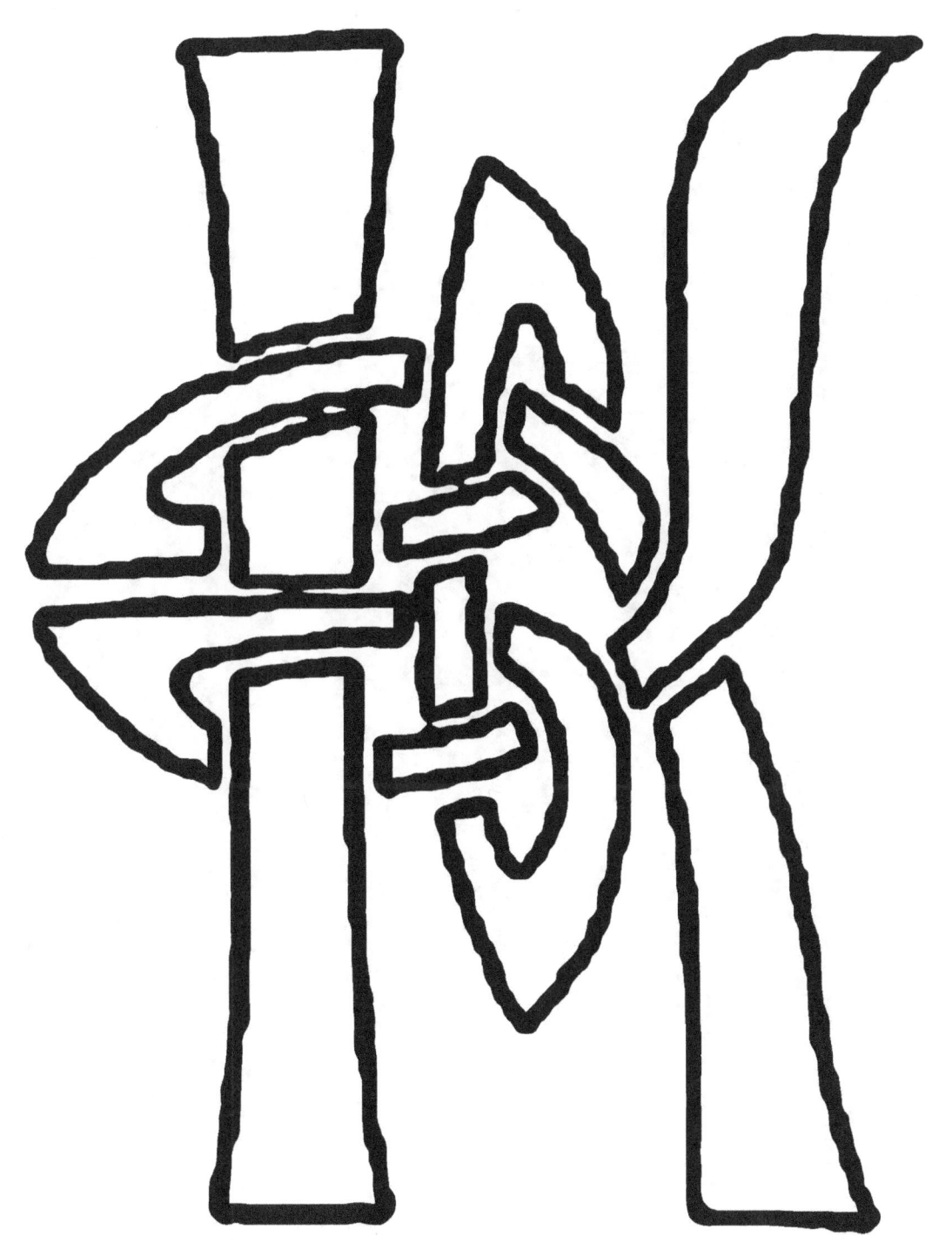

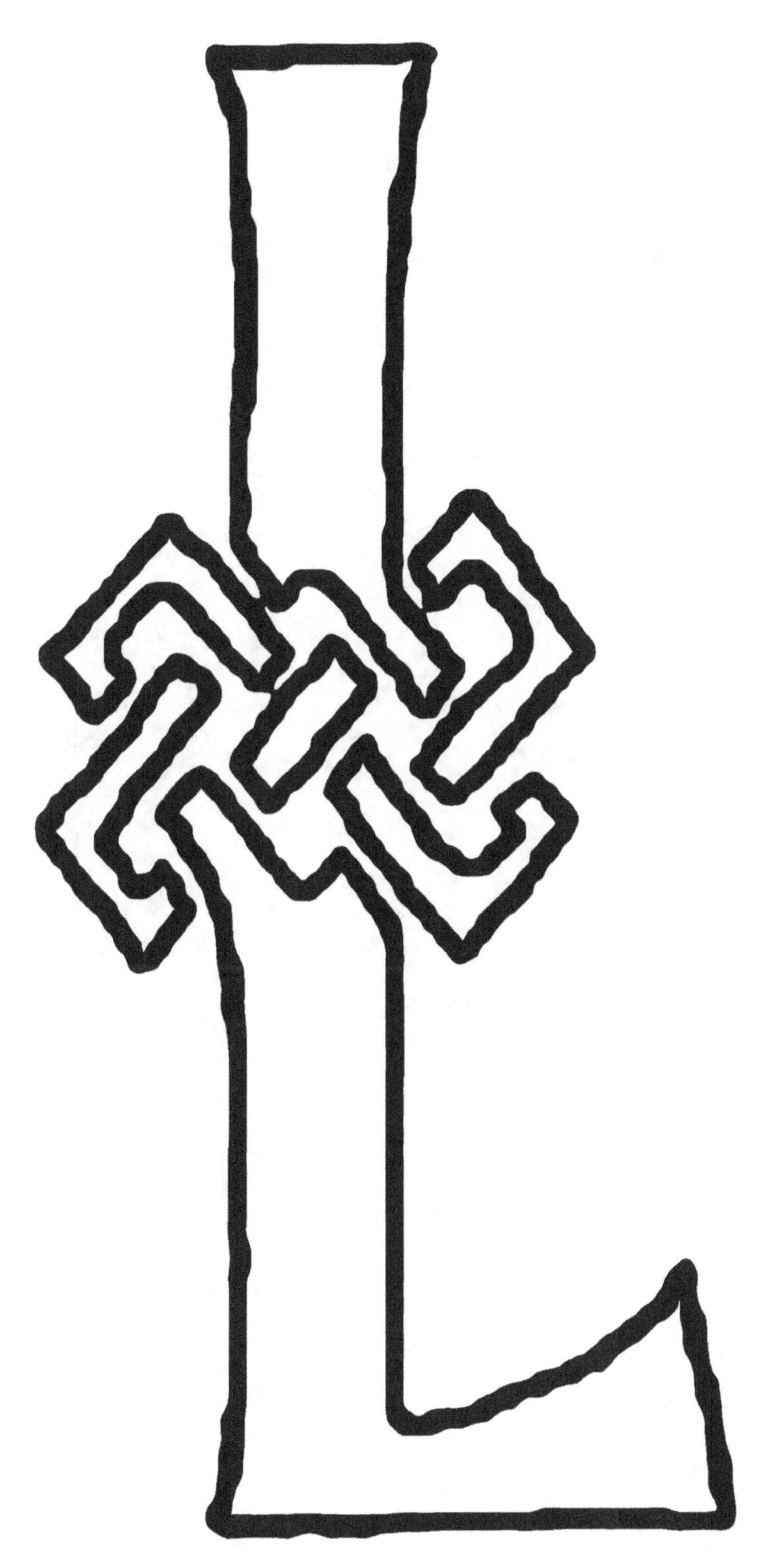

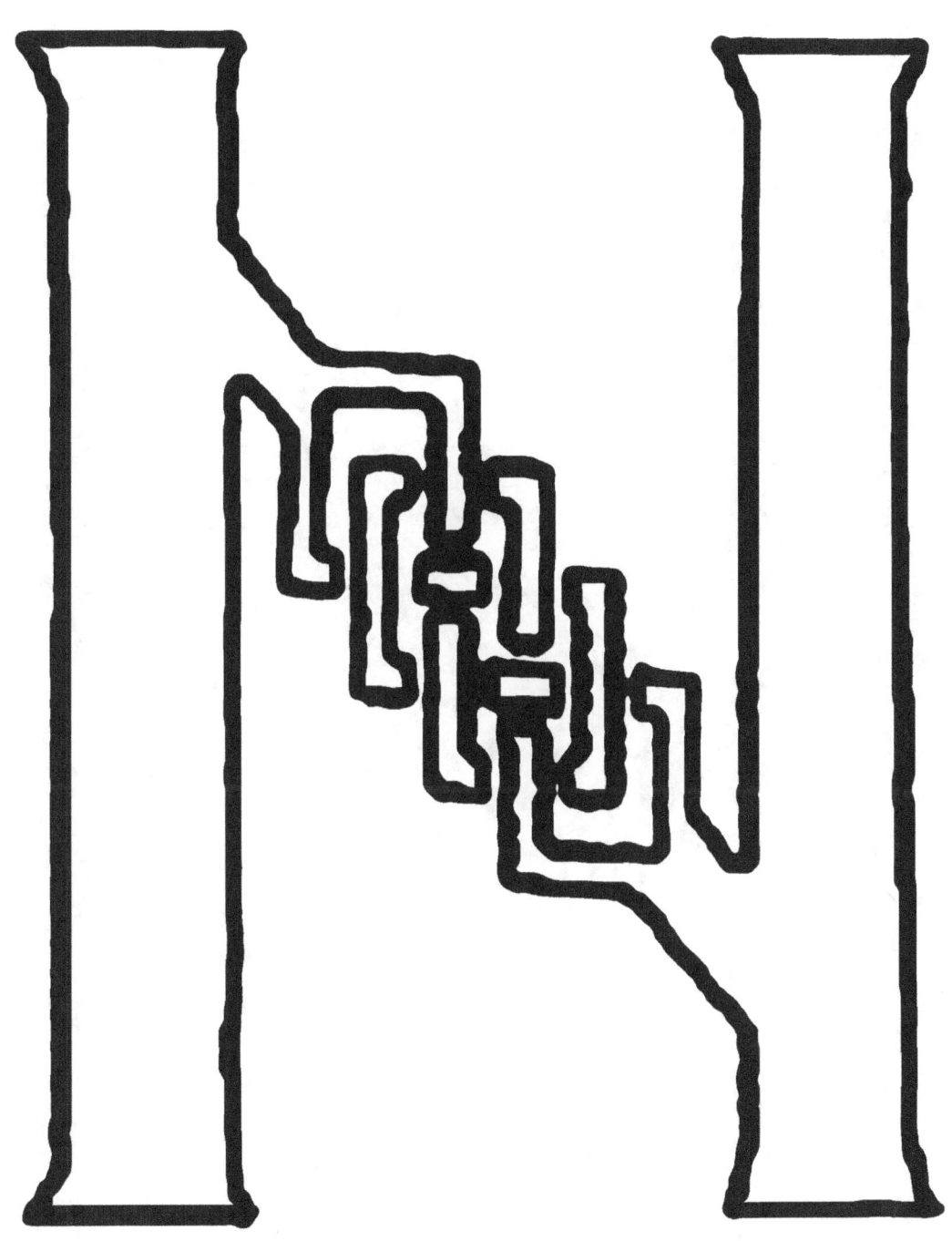

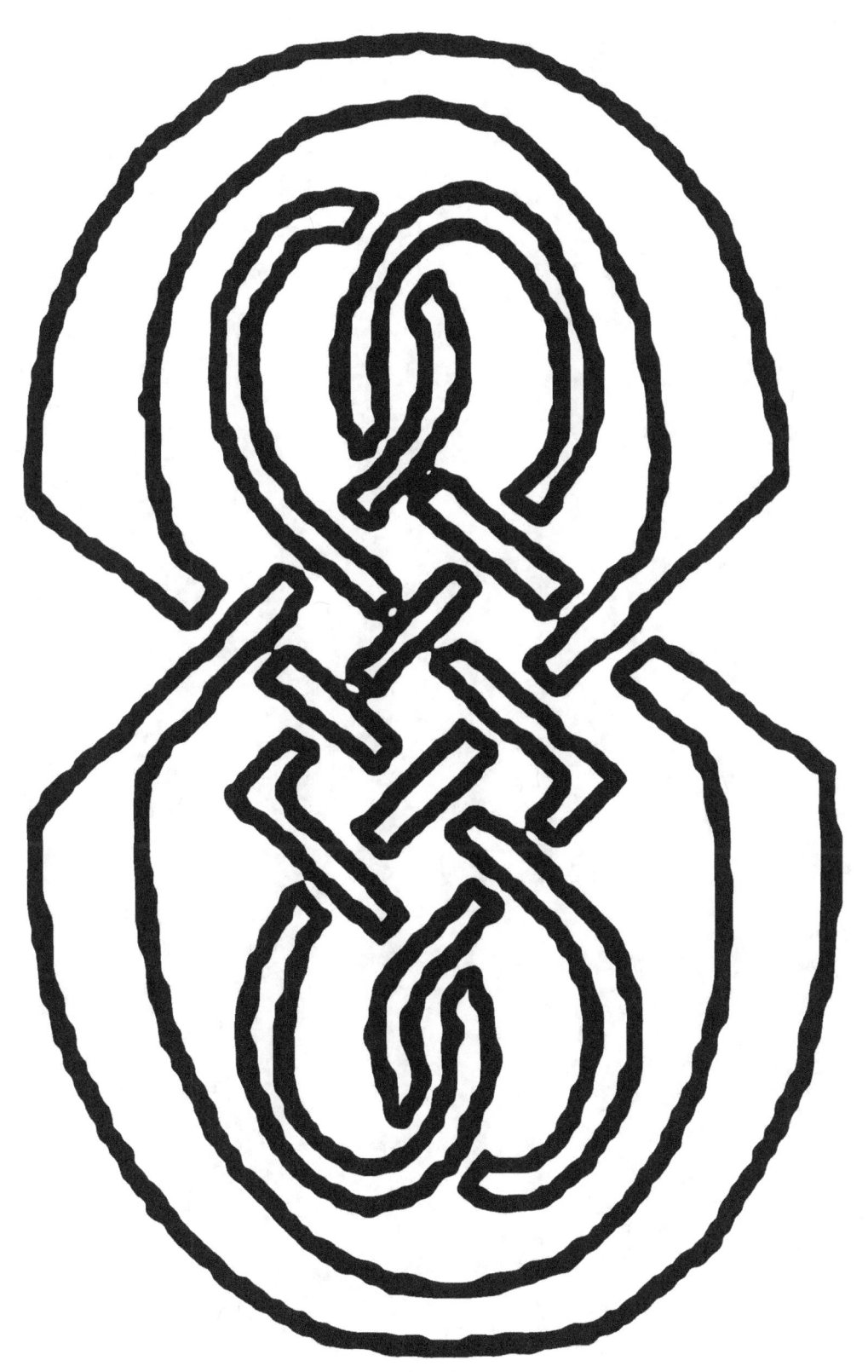

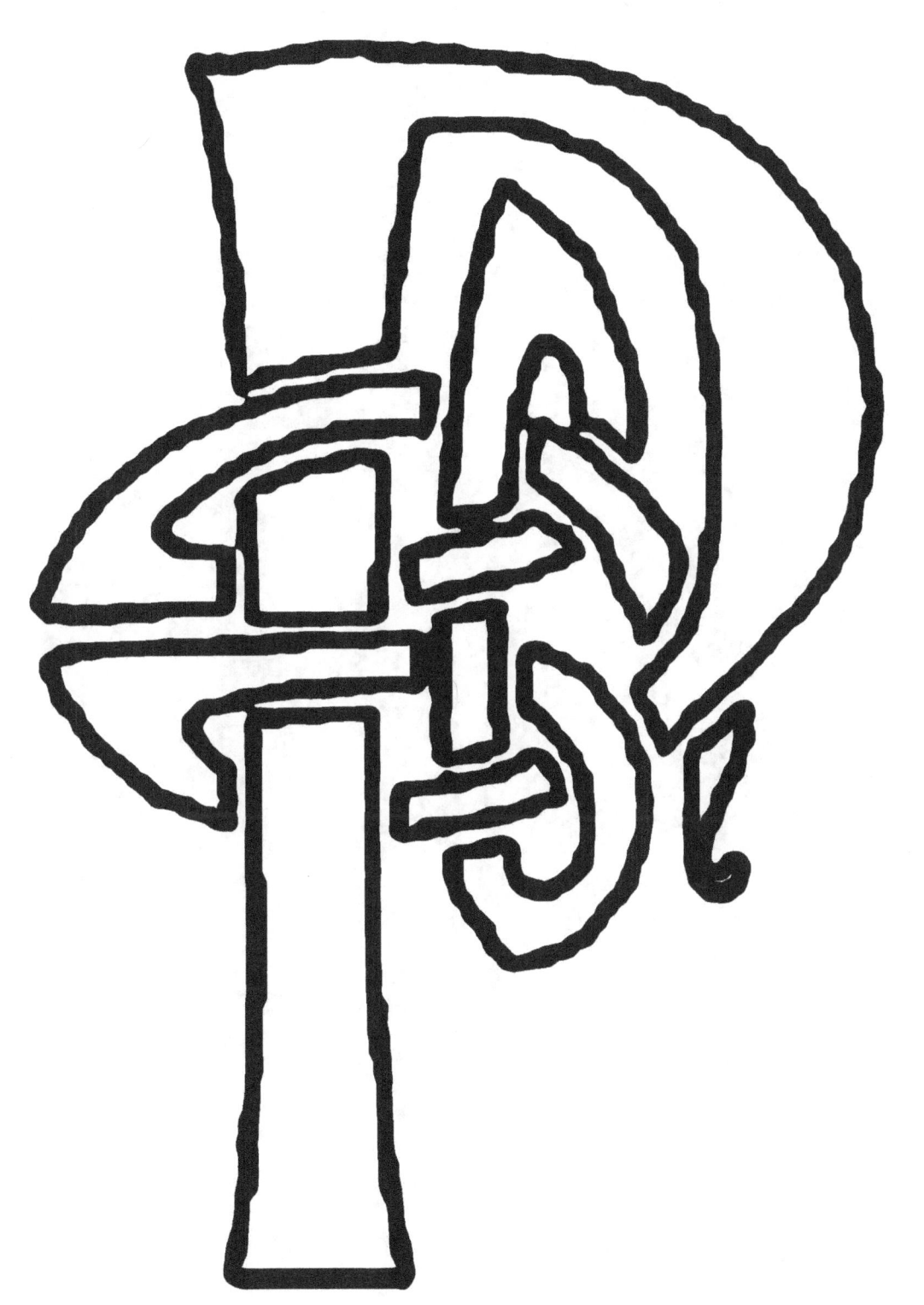

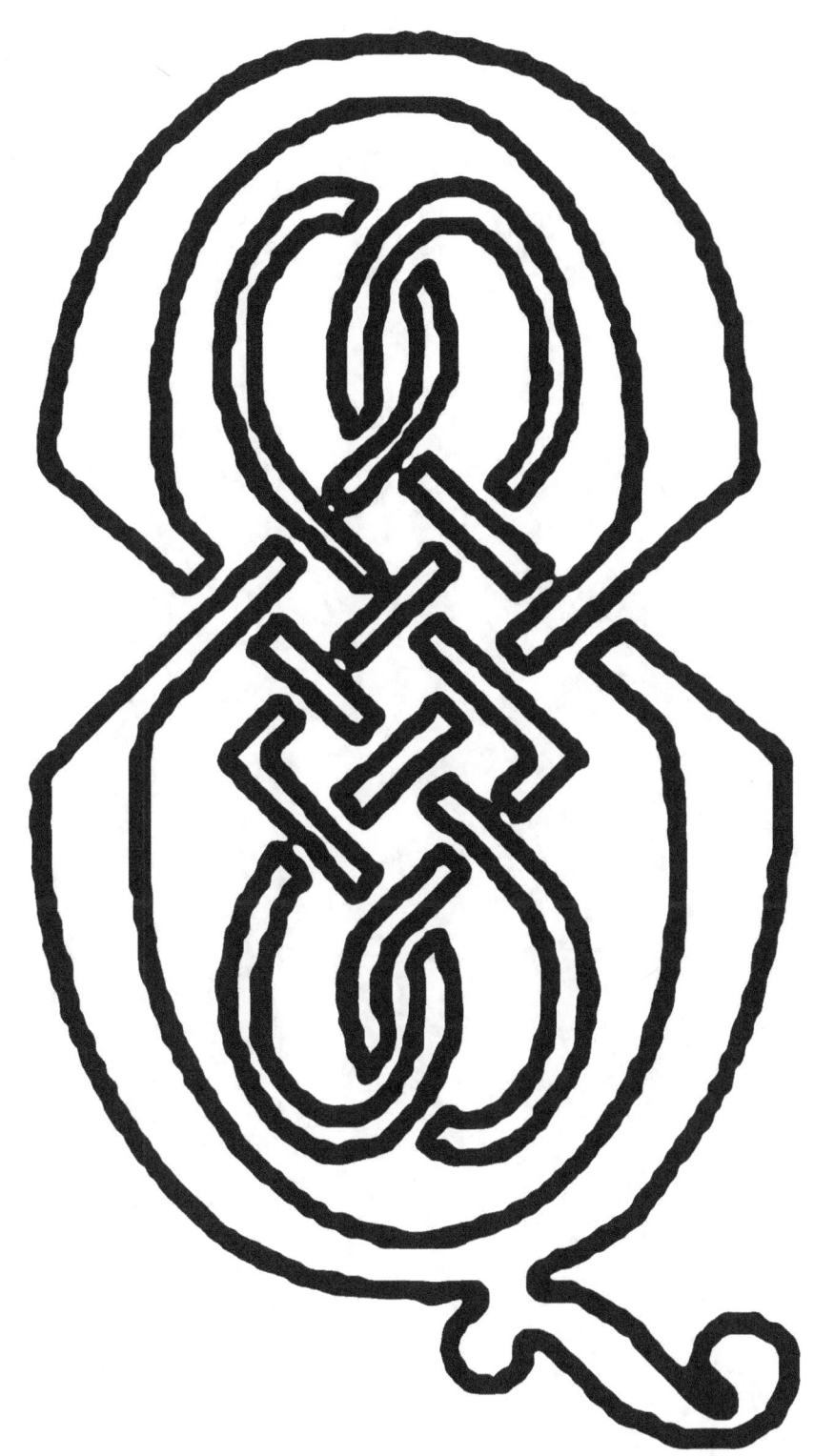

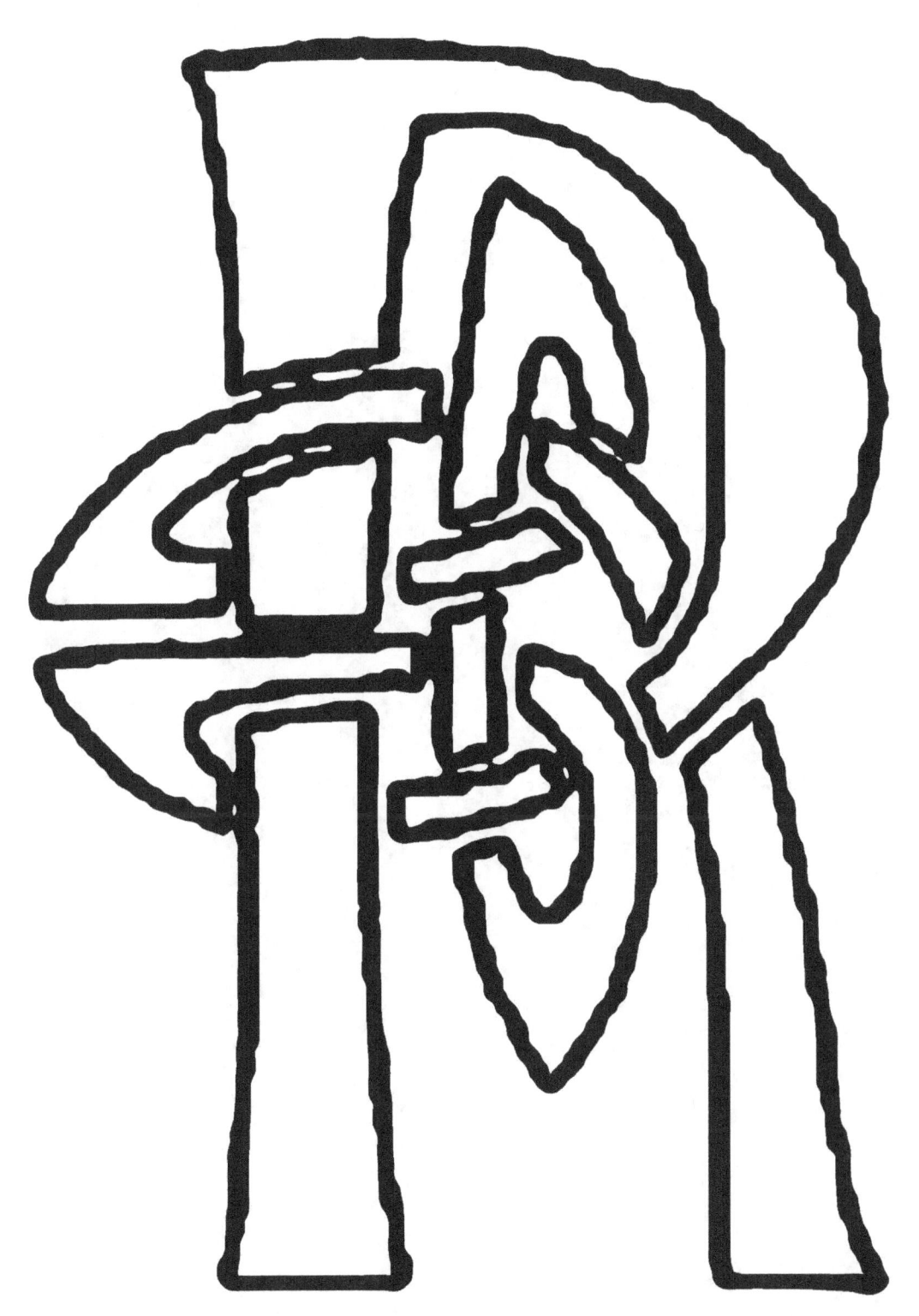

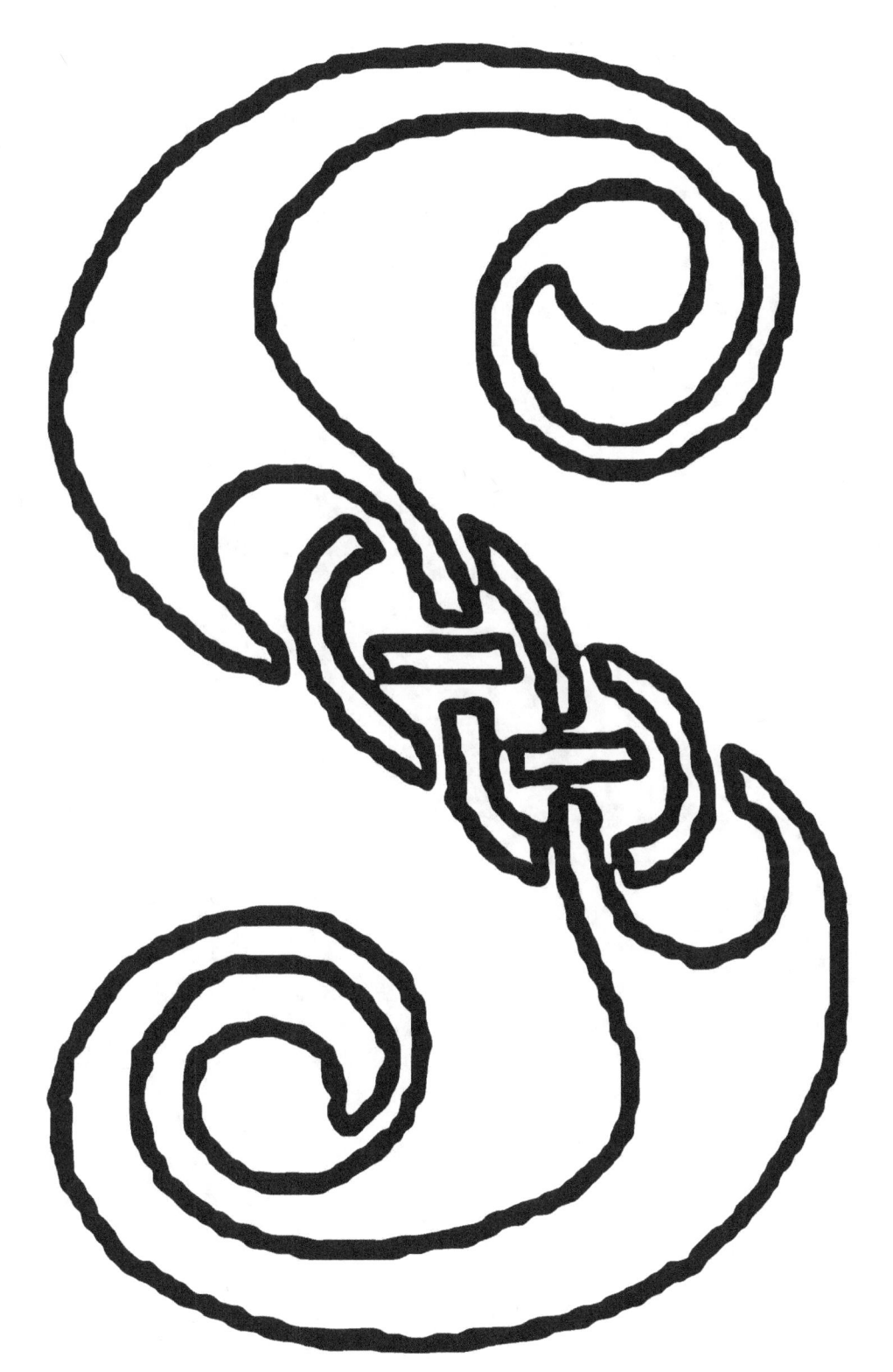

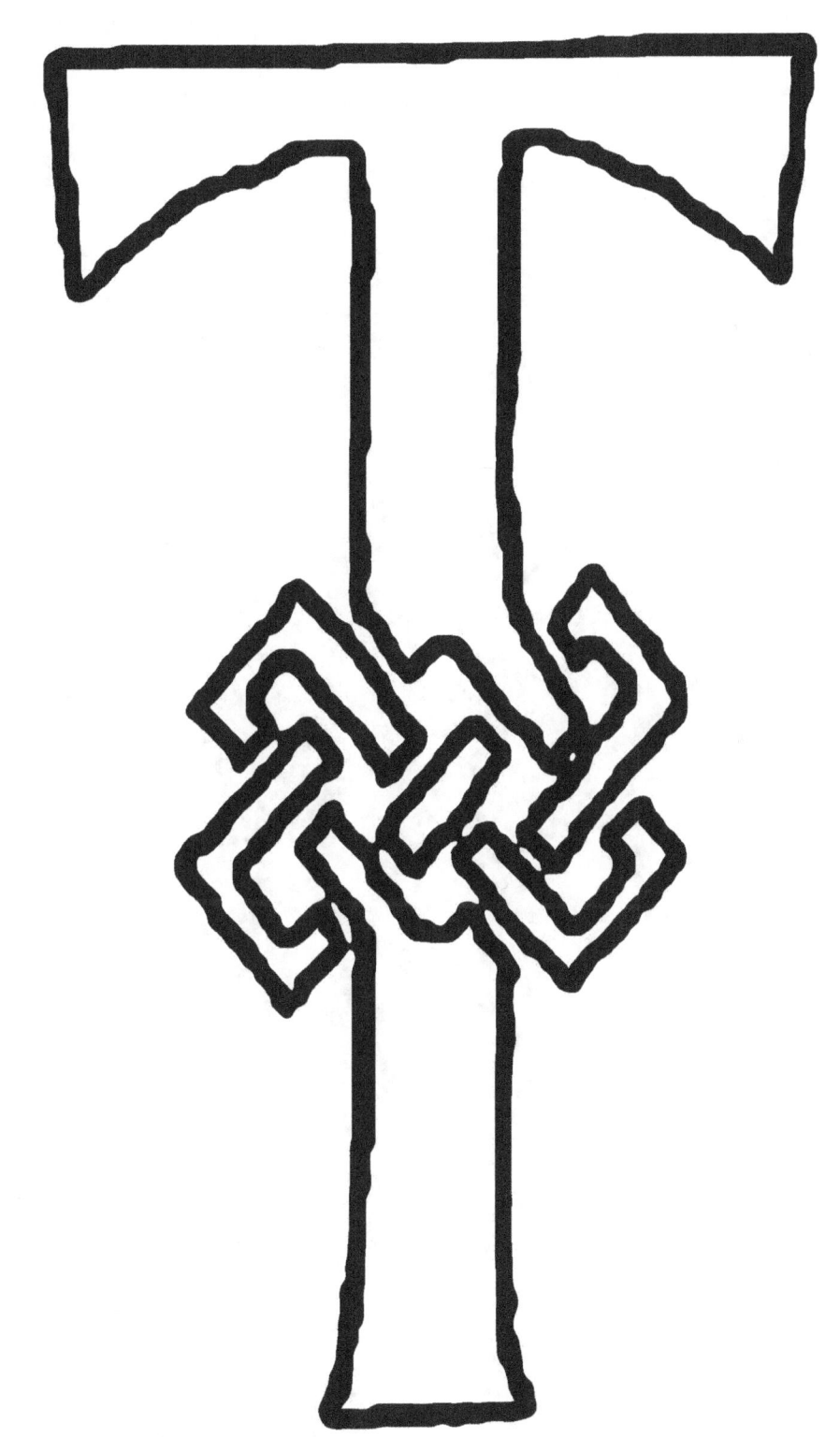

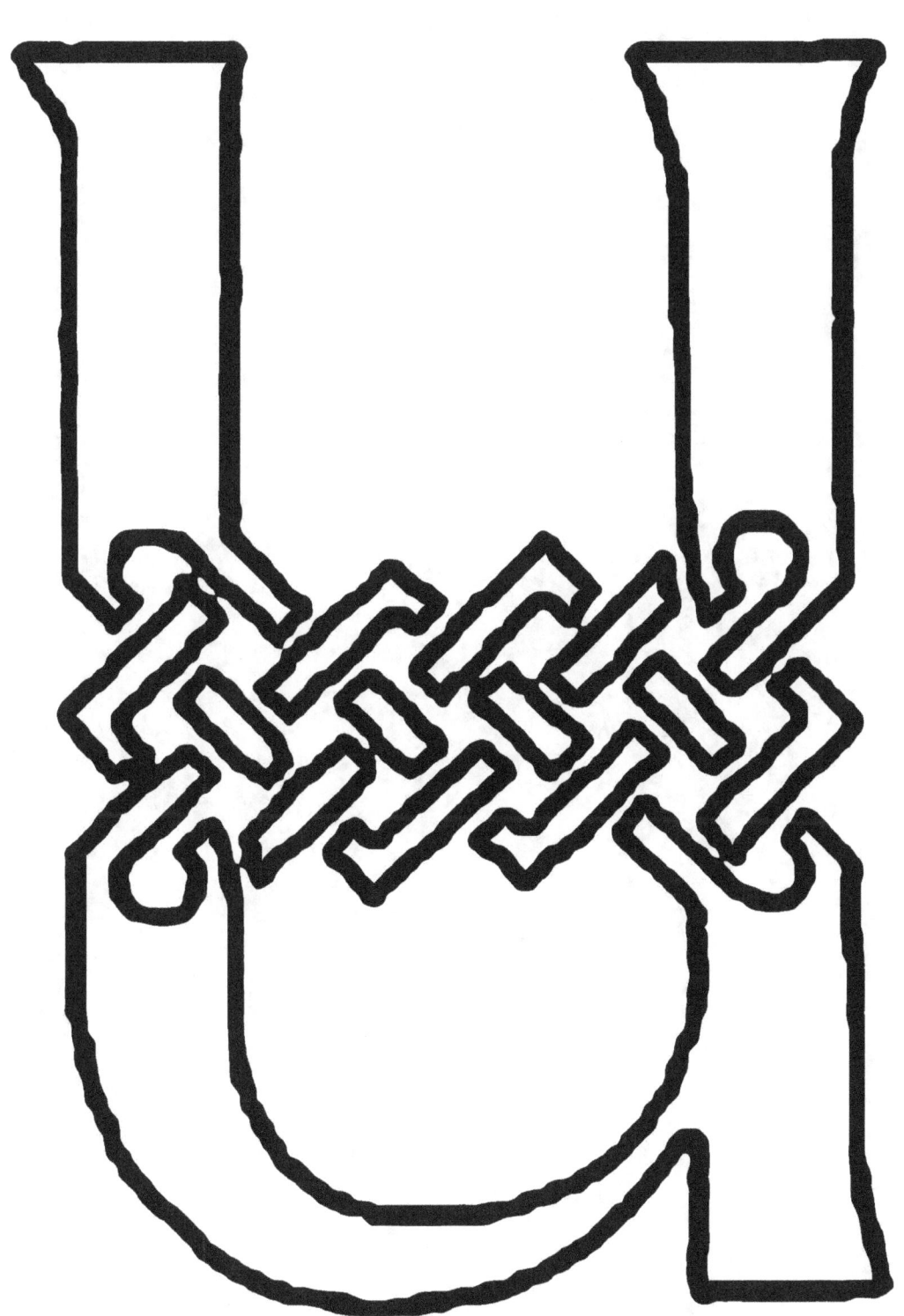

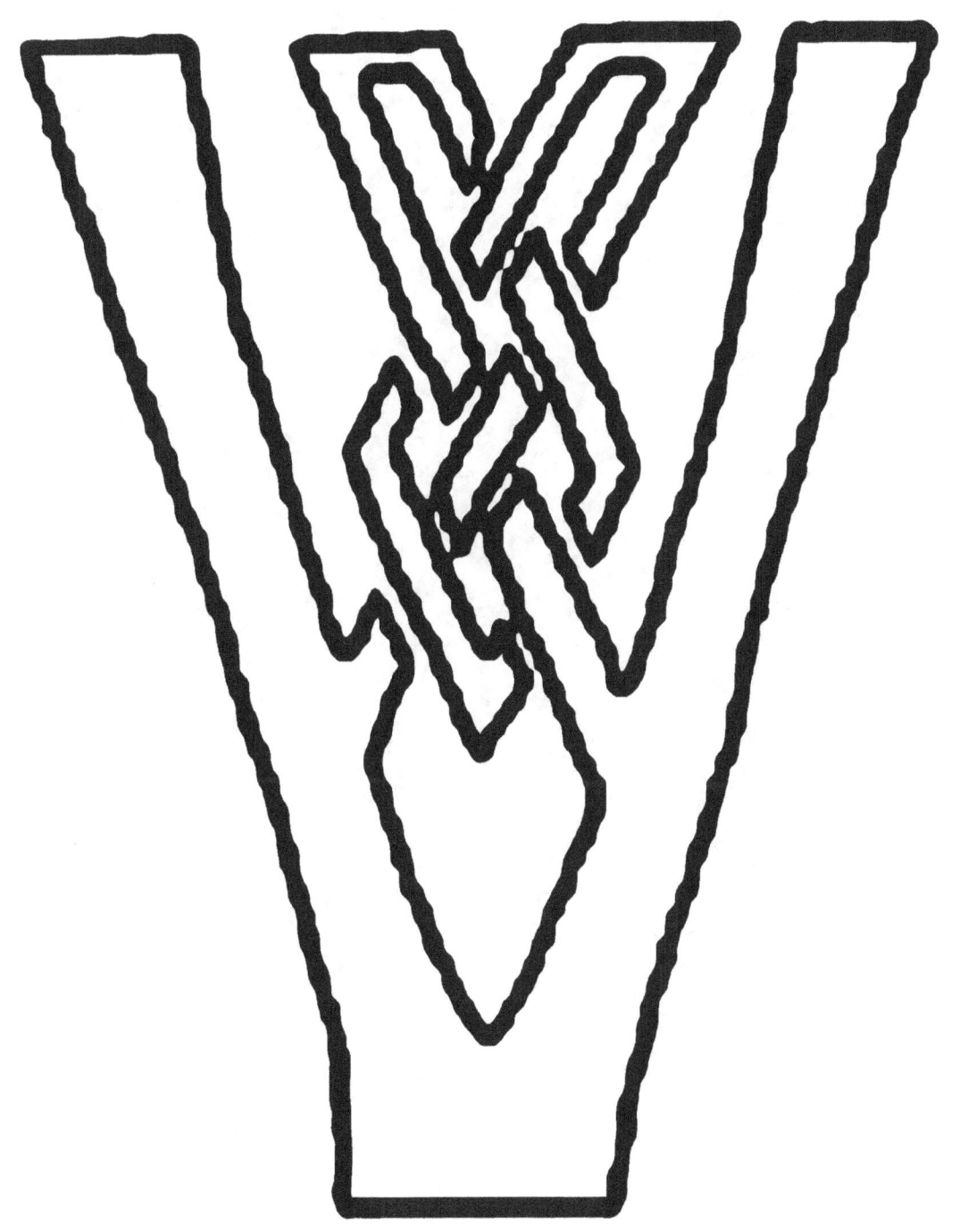

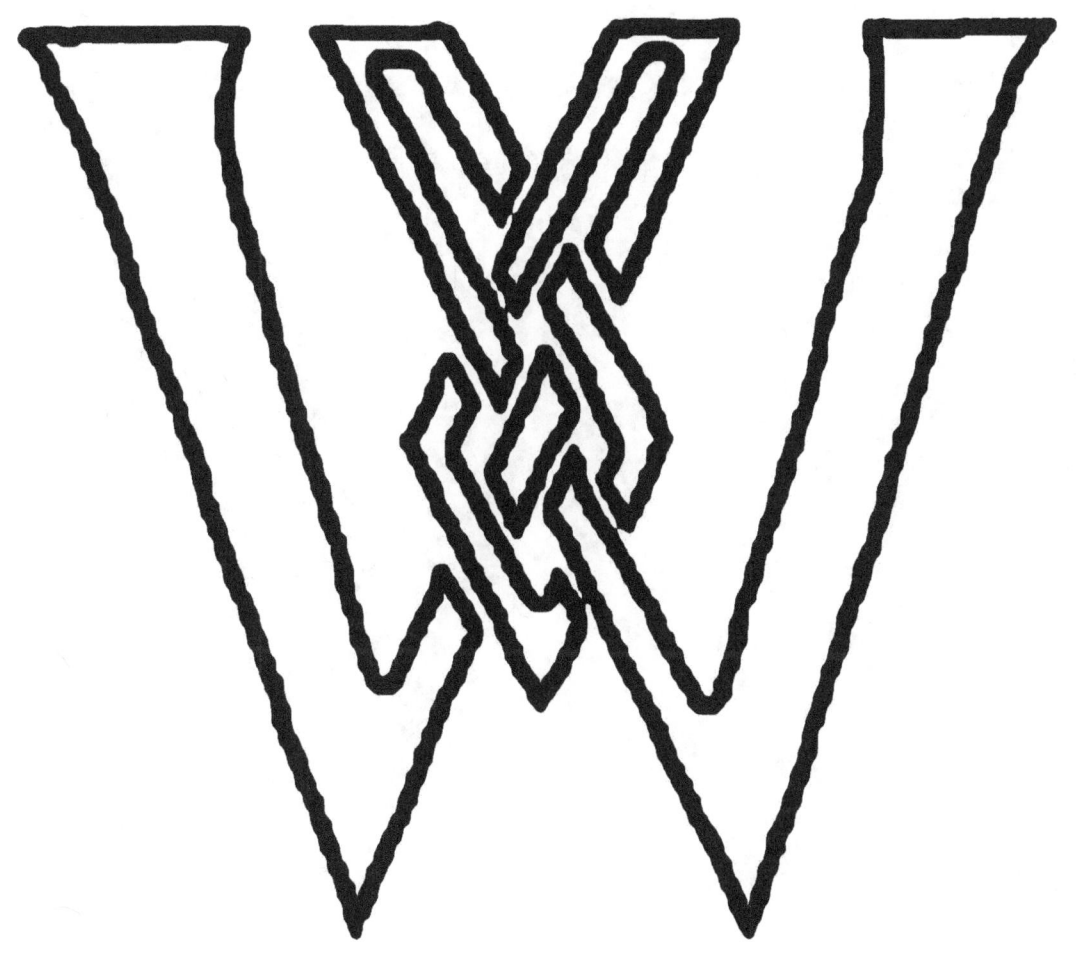

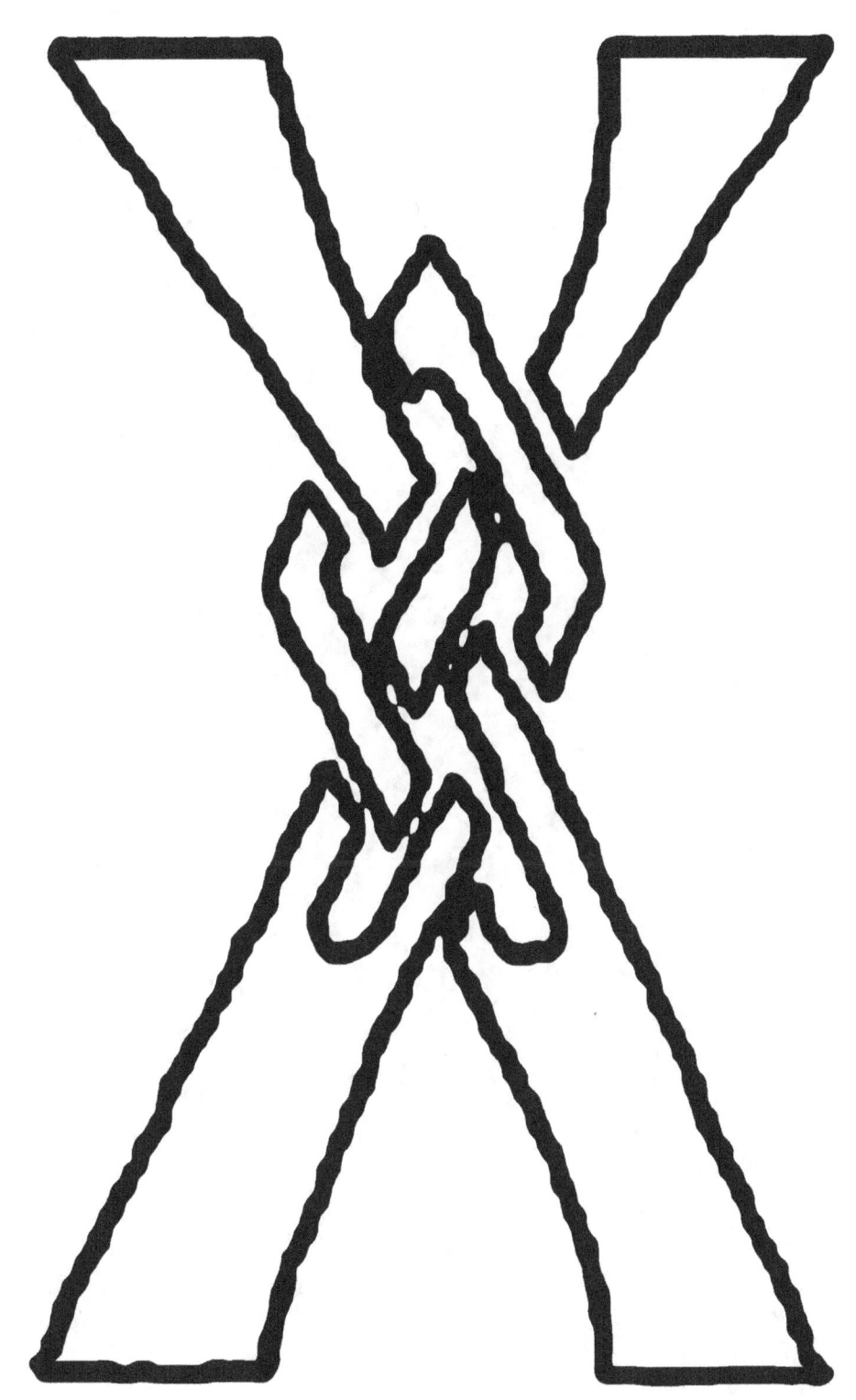

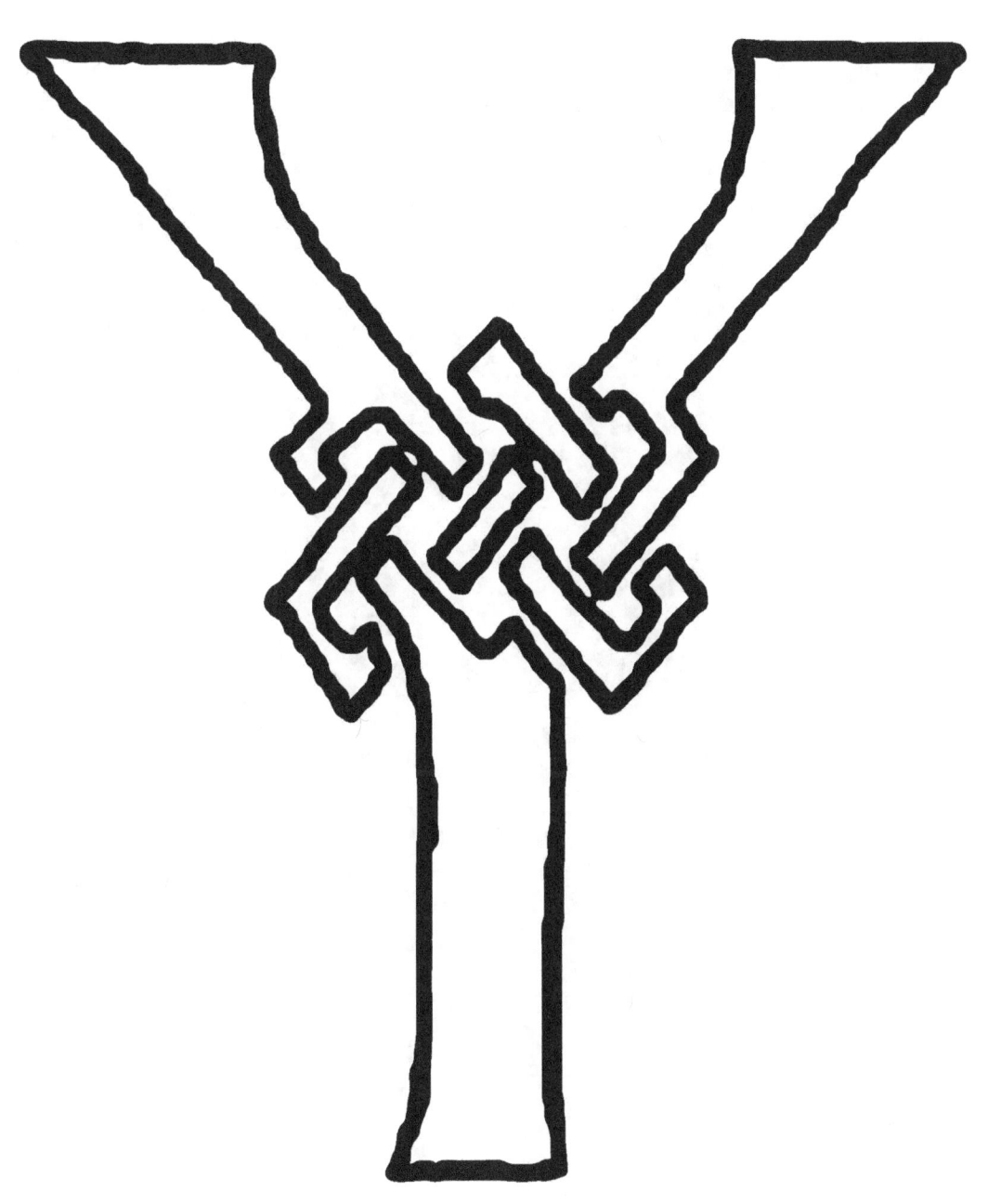

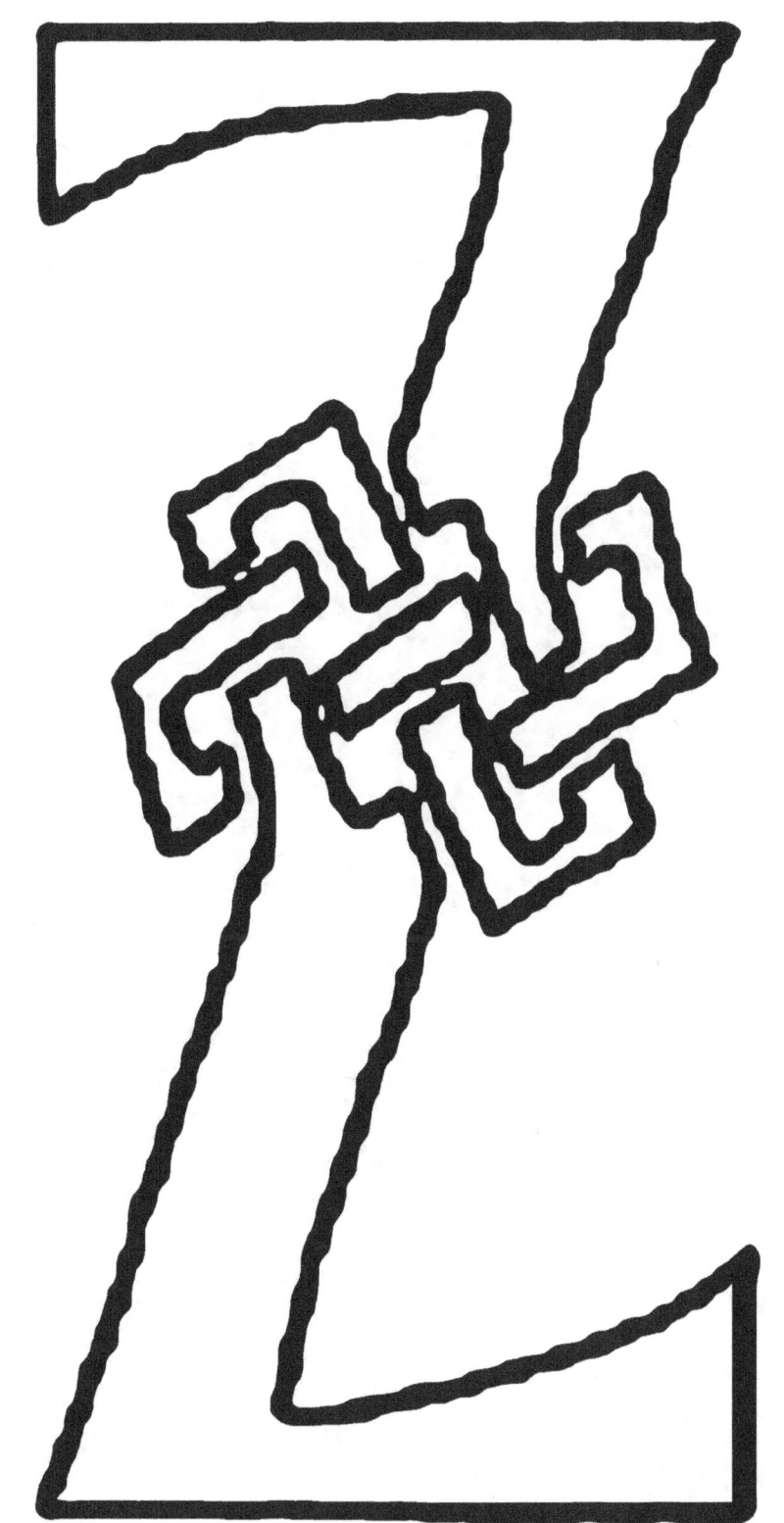

Hi there, my name is Jeff.

I hope you enjoyed this coloring book.

These coloring books are available for immediate download in my etsy shop-jfstudioshop.

If you would like to download individual images don't hesitate to check it out.